PUFFIN BOOKS

Good Enough to Eat

Roger McGough is one of Britain's most popular poets. He has been captivating children and adults alike with his unique blend of compassion and wit for more than three decades and with more than thirty books. He is an international ambassador for poetry and was awarded an OBE for his work in 1997. In 2001 he was honoured with the Freedom of the City of Liverpool.

Roger McGough

Good Enough to Eat

Illustrated by
Lydia Monks

PUFFIN BOOKS

For Mathew and Isabel

PUFFIN BOOKS

Published by the Penguin Group
Penguin Books Ltd, 80 Strand, London WC2R 0RL, England
Penguin Putnam Inc., 375 Hudson Street, New York, New York 10014, USA
Penguin Books Australia Ltd, 250 Camberwell Road, Camberwell, Victoria 3124, Australia
Penguin Books Canada Ltd, 10 Alcorn Avenue, Toronto, Ontario, Canada M4V 3B2
Penguin Books India (P) Ltd, 11 Community Centre, Panchsheel Park, New Delhi – 110 017, India
Penguin Books (NZ) Ltd, Cnr Rosedale and Airborne Roads, Albany, Auckland, New Zealand
Penguin Books (South Africa) (Pty) Ltd, 24 Sturdee Avenue, Rosebank 2196, South Africa

Penguin Books Ltd, Registered Offices: 80 Strand, London WC2R 0RL, England

www.penguin.com

First published 2002
2

Set in Bembo 13/15pt

Made and printed in England by Clays Ltd, St Ives plc

British Library Cataloguing in Publication Data
A CIP catalogue record for this book is available from the British Library

ISBN 0–141–31494–X

Contents

Good Enough to Eat

This poem looks scrumptious
This poem looks great
I wish I had a poem like this
Each morning on my plate

This poem looks tasty
This poem looks sweet
And if it's good enough to publish
Then it's good enough to eat

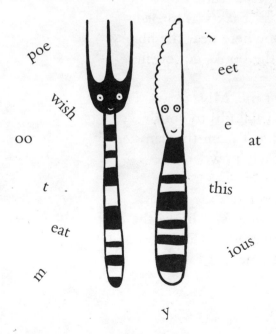

It Wasn't Me, Miss

It wasn't me, Miss, it was 'er, Miss
Every lesson it's the same
I never do nothin'
But I always get the blame

I didn't smash that window
Or throw water on the floor
It wasn't me who put the frog
In Mrs Kelly's drawer

I didn't make rude noises
When yer back was turned
I was nowhere near the library
When the books got burned

It wasn't me, Miss, it was 'er, Miss
Would I tell fibs to you?
An' I didn't paint the hamster
That lovely powder blue

I didn't scratch the piano
It wasn't me who broke the chair
And any road, if I did
It wasn't me, it was 'er

She acts all sweet and innocent
But the minute that you're gone
She's *Frankenstein* and *Reservoir Dogs*
All rolled into one.

It wasn't me, Miss, it was 'er, Miss
… What? … Sit apart?
Don't be mean, Miss, we're a team, Miss
I'll be good, cross my heart!

Fourteen Lines
(Not a Sonnet)

I must not talk in class
I must not walk in class
I must not walk on the grass
I must not chalk on the grass
I must not choke on the gas
I must not smoke on the bus
I must not bark at a puss
I must not squawk through the glass
I must not gawk at a lass
I must not talk, alas
I must not talk
I must not
I must
I

Rules

1) Which came first, the rule or the ruler?

2) Either way, you, the ruled, came last.

3) Rulers come and go, we don't.

4) Remember that.

5) Remember this, rules are the spaces between the bars of a cage.

6) Break the rules and the rules will break you.

7) Rules enjoy the company of other rules.

8) We have long, long memories.

9) What was number 4?

10) Sit up and pay attention.

What I Love About School

What I love about school
       is the hurly-burly of the classroom,
       the sly humour of the teachers

What I hate about teachers
       is their reluctance to cartwheel
       down corridors

What I love about corridors
       is that the longer they are
       the louder the echo

What I hate about echo echo
       is its refusal to answer a straight
       question question

What I love about question
       is the proud admission
       of its own ignorance

What I hate about ignorance
       is the naive assumption
       that it is bliss

What I love about bliss
       is its willingness
       to rhyme with kiss

What I hate about kiss
      is the news of it going around
      like wildfire

What I love about wildfire
      is its dragon's breath
      and its hunger for life

What I hate about life
      is that as soon as you get the hang of it
      you run out of time

What I love about time
      is how it flies
      except when at school

What I hate about school
      is the hurly-burly of the playground,
      the sly humour of the teachers.

Head

The Head of our school
is called Mr Head.
Honestly, that's his name.

'My name is Head
and I'm the new Head,'
Is what he said when he came.

He's very, very nice
but it has to be said,
that our Head, Mr Head,
has a very large head.

It says 'Head' on his sports bag,
and 'Head' on the door,
but which of the heads
does the 'Head' stand for?

The Boy with a Similar Name

When Raymond Gough joined our class
He was almost a year behind.
'Sanatorium,' said Mrs McBride
'So I want you all to be kind.'

'Roger, your names are similar
So let Raymond sit next to you
He'll need a friend to teach him the ropes
And show him what to do.'

Then teacher went back to teaching
And we went back to being taught
And I tried to be kind to Raymond
But it was harder than I thought.

For he was the colour of candlewax
And smelled of Dettol and Vick.
He was as thin as a sharpened pencil
And his glasses were milk-bottle thick.

Not only that but unfriendly
All muffled up in his shell.
Hobbies? Interests? Ambitions?
It was impossible to tell.

I was afraid of catching his yellowness
And smelling of second-hand Vick
And the only time I could be myself
Were the days when he was off sick.

But what proved to be contagious
Was his oddness, and I knew
That he was a victim ripe for bullying
And so by proxy, I was too.

'How's your brother Raymond?'
The class began to tease,
'Do you share his dirty handkerchief?
Do you catch each other's fleas?'

'He's not my brother,' I shouted,
My cheeks all burning hot,
'He's a drippy four-eyed monster,
And he comes from the planet Snot.'

They laughed and I saw an opening
(Wouldn't you have done the same?)
I pointed a finger at Raymond
And joined in the bullying game.

He stopped coming to school soon after,
'Sanatorium,' said Mrs McBride.
He never came back and nobody knew
If he moved elsewhere or died.

I don't think of him very often
For when I do I blush with shame
At the thought of the pain I helped inflict
On the boy with a similar name.

Reward and Punishment

If you are very good I will give you:

A pillow of blue strawberries
A swimming pool of Haagen Das
A mirror of imagination
A pocketful of yes's
A hiss of sleigh rides
A lunch box of swirling planets
A doorway of happy endings
A hedgerow of diamonds
A surfboard of dolphins
A cat's paw of tickles
A carton of fresh rainbow-juice
A forest of chocolate wardrobes

If you are naughty you will get:

A burst of balloon
A screech of wolf
A hoof of piggy bank
A twitch of sideways
A splinter of thirst
A precipice of banana skins
A tyrannosaurus of broccoli
A rucksack of bony elbows
A skeleton of lost pencils
A flag of inconvenience
A chill of false laughter
A blackboard of no way out

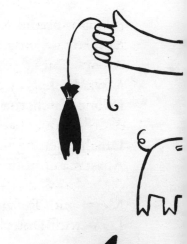

Gap Year

Lavinia is leaving for Slovenia
Saskia is off to Nebraska

Olivia is bound for Bolivia
Miranda is going to Uganda

Maria backpacks in Korea
Dilly on a charter to Chile

Dinah is jetting to China
Anastasia en route for Malaysia

Meryl with Beryl in Kerala
Lotte with Dotty in Lanzarote

Blanche with her aunts in Provence
Ann with a man in Turkestan

Eunice has turned up in Tunis
Carly's gone native in Bali

Laetitia fishes in Mauritius
Cecily's sunning in Sicily

Dan's in Iran, Zak's in Iraq
Pete's in Crete, Noah's in Goa

Dennis in Venice, Shona, Verona
Elaine's in Maine … Oh God, what a pain.

One's chums have all flown the coop
One's left here alone. Will one cope?

Tea Leaves

Some people read papers and magazines
Others prefer cartoons and comics
Some read manuals about how things work
A few study Home Economics

Some eagerly devour those I-Spy books
That classify flowers and birds
While others, big, fat dictionaries
That give the meanings of words

But old Mrs Lee, when she wants to read
Then this is what she'll do
Boil the kettle, warm the pot
And make a nice fresh brew

For old Mrs Lee reads tea leaves
And as soon as she gets up
It's toast and a chair by the window
Then cup after cup after cup

Of fables, folklore and legends
Of memoirs and novels of course
Of sci-fi, thrillers, romances
Of sagas from Aga to Norse

All the tales that have ever been written
All the characters, places and plots
The information stored away
In the leaves like microdots

And so late into the evening
While her neighbours are watching TV
Mrs Lee is still there, cat on her lap
With a book in a nice cup of tea.

READING
IS A PLEASURE
THAT MOST OF US
TAKE FOR GRANTED
IMAGINE THE CHALLENGE OF
HAVING TO WORK REALLY HARD
toreadandmakesenseoftheworld.

To read and make sense of the world.

To read.

Trapped!

The tendrils of the night drift down.
The moon silvers the mountain-side
urging the tide to turn, and like
a barracuda, attack the helpless
shoreline. *HELP! HELP! I'M SUFFOCATING!*
Moonbeams, gleaming and radiant,
glisten and, like shards of desire,
lift the gentle breeze *I'M TRAPPED*
IN THE MIDDLE OF A TERRIBLE POEM!
that fingers the darkening motes
of my mind. *I'M DROWNING ...*
Soon the dawn *IN CLICHÉS*
will creep in on rose-coloured toes
and pulling back the dull curtain
of anxiety reveal a brilliant,
new world, where all is peace.
AAAGGGHHHH!

Sound Advice

Once you write a poem
You must write another

To prevent the first
From falling over.

New Poem

So far, so good

Writer's Block

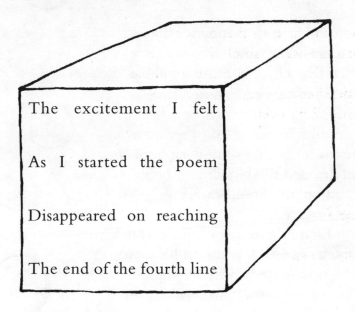

The excitement I felt

As I started the poem

Disappeared on reaching

The end of the fourth line

Executioner's Block

Money good
Hours short
Can't stand blood
Don't like sport

Had to stop
Nervous wreck
Given chop
Pain in neck.

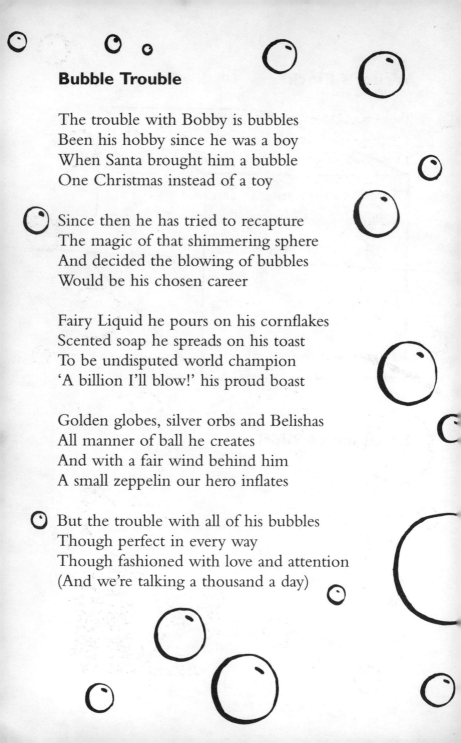

Bubble Trouble

The trouble with Bobby is bubbles
Been his hobby since he was a boy
When Santa brought him a bubble
One Christmas instead of a toy

Since then he has tried to recapture
The magic of that shimmering sphere
And decided the blowing of bubbles
Would be his chosen career

Fairy Liquid he pours on his cornflakes
Scented soap he spreads on his toast
To be undisputed world champion
'A billion I'll blow!' his proud boast

Golden globes, silver orbs and Belishas
All manner of ball he creates
And with a fair wind behind him
A small zeppelin our hero inflates

But the trouble with all of his bubbles
Though perfect in every way
Though fashioned with love and attention
(And we're talking a thousand a day)

These incandescent flotillas
These gravitational blips
These would-be orbiting planets
Within seconds of leaving his lips

Go *POP!* Just like that

At Three and a Half

On waking, he collides with the bedroom.
His bunny-rabbit slippers are unusual
in that they clatter on the thick carpet.

When he finishes with the bathroom
it is a wet rag, echoing still
to the sound of soap bubbles exploding.

Breakfast is not for the faint-hearted.
Born to outshout the opposition,
he practises on cereals that answer back.

Armed with a banana, he blasts his way
down the hall, before engaging
the jacket-monster in mortal combat.

When he leaves with a slam, the house
takes its hand from its ears, and silence
sits and fidgets like an unwelcome visitor.

Mums and Dads

My daddy's a lawyer
said Mort
He wears a wig when he goes to court

So does my mum
said Allister
And her wig's big cos she's a barrister

My dad drives a truck
said Gus
As wide as a playground as big as a bus

My mum's a chef
said Jocasta
She bakes her own bread and makes her own pasta

My daddy's a doctor
said Henrietta
He gives people pills to make them feel better

My mum's a model
said Rose
And she gets to keep all her beautiful clothes

My dad's a boxer
said Lee
So you'd better think twice before picking on me

My mum's a footballer
said Jane
And next week she's playing for England again

My dad's a runner
said Sid
Well that's what my mum said he did

My mum's a mum
said Sue
With three sons and five daughters what else
    can she do?

My dad's a tattooist
said Liam
And Mum's got the crown jewels where no one
    can see 'em

My mum's a vicar
said Tessa
She works every day, even Sundays, God bless her

My dad's a detective
said Isabel
Though to look at him you couldn't tell

My mum's a dietician
said Gaby
She shouts at ladies when they get flabby

My dad's unemployed
said Eliza
Though he used to be a careers' adviser.

A Domesticated Donkey

A domesticated donkey from Slough
Wished to knit a new jumper but how?
   Attempts with her ears
   Resulted in tears
So instead, she knitted her brow.

The Perfect Present

What I wanted at the age of ONE
Was a rattle to shake and chew upon

What I got at the age of ONE
Was a brick with rattle painted on

What I wanted at the age of TWO
Was a teddy bear, faithful and true

What I got at the age of TWO
Was a piece of fur and a stick of glue

What I wanted at the age of THREE
Was a tricycle as new as can be

What I got at the age of THREE
Was a pair of pram wheels nailed to a tree

What I wanted at the age of FOUR
Was a fearsome, gruesome dinosaur

What I got at the age of FOUR
Was a plastic lobster with only one claw

What I wanted at the age of FIVE
Was a silver kite to swoop and dive

What I got at the age of FIVE
Was a homeless pigeon more dead than alive

What I wanted at the age of SIX
Was a magic wand and a box of tricks

What I got at the age of SIX
Was a pair of granny's walking sticks

What I wanted at the age of SEVEN
Was a racing car, battery driven

What I got at the age of SEVEN
Was a beer mat from a pub in Devon

What I wanted at the age of EIGHT
Was a surfboard, wouldn't that be great?

What I got at the age of EIGHT
Was a swimming ring that wouldn't inflate

What I wanted at the age of NINE
Was a fishing rod with reel and line

What I got at the age of NINE
Was a safety pin and a ball of twine

What I wanted at the age of TEN
Was a diary and a fountain pen

At the age of TEN
Dad won the lottery. Bought me Disneyland.

Couch Potato

When I watch TV
I always slouch

So I bought myself
A potato couch.

The Great I Am

I am
the great
I am

I am
in bed at
I am

sametimedotcom

(A really useful website)

Learn how to clean out the hamster cage
And improve your language skills
At the same time!

Learn how to mend a bicycle puncture
And play the saxophone
At the same time!

Learn how to bake chocolate brownies
And strengthen your tennis serve
At the same time!

Learn how to tap dance
And study the movement of the planets
At the same time!

Learn how to rub your tummy in a circular
    motion (with one hand)
And the top of your head (with the other)
At the same time!

Famous Inventions

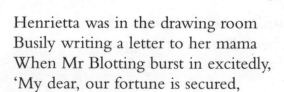

Blotting Paper

Henrietta was in the drawing room
Busily writing a letter to her mama
When Mr Blotting burst in excitedly,
'My dear, our fortune is secured,

I have invented a new kind of napkin
That will absorb soup and gravy stains.'
'Oh, Henry,' she cried, 'look what you've done,
Made me spill ink all over the notepaper!'

Sunglasses

'Ray, your eye-glasses are completely coated
With charcoal dust,' laughed Mrs Bann.
'I know, mother, although strangely enough
I didn't notice when I was out in the garden
Barbecuing burgers in the noonday sun.'

Toast

'Oh, thou stupid boy,' said Mistress Toast
To young Egbert. 'Thou hast dropped
A slice of bread straight on to ye fire.'

'Never mind, mother, I will fork it out
And coat it thickly with butter to mask
Ye burned taste … mmm, delicious.'

Two Riddles

(i)

Identical twins
We live on opposite sides
Of a hill that is not steep.
Yet we never see each other.
Yes, we sometimes weep.

(ii)

Though I am blind
You can count on me to show you the way.
Deaf to the noise of traffic, which is just as well
For the side of a busy road is where I dwell.
Once I was sought after, but now ignored
I have become my own headstone.
I am old and growing bored.

Bird on a Wire

Blame the starlings
the lights have gone out

Blame the leaves
the trains can't run

Blame the sun
the wind and the sea

But whatever you do
Don't blame me.

('The village was without electricity for nearly five hours after a
huge flock of starlings settled on overhead high tension lines and
the wire was twisted under their weight – *Salisbury Journal*, 28
October 1999)

The Case of the Vanishing Cathedral

Wednesday night was windy and wet
And one that Salisbury will never forget
For the cathedral vanished without a trace
Has it been kidnapped or sucked into space?

The police confess they have drawn a blank
Was it the work of the devil, or a student prank?
No ransom note, no clues to be found
No sign of a struggle, just a hole in the ground.

His Grace, the Bishop, sees it as a sign
Of retribution at the hand of the Divine
A millennium warning as clear as day
For Christians to get on their knees and pray.

The Chamber of Commerce, of course, is dismayed
For what will become of the tourist trade?
(Although *X-Files* fanatics may all flock to see
The spot where the cathedral used to be.)

In the Town Hall, however, planners have planned
How best to make use of this prime piece of land
Green campaigners may go into shock
On seeing the new car park, an eight-storey block.

I don't mean to alarm, for I'm just as perplexed
But keep an eye on Stonehenge,
It may well be next.

Zebra Crossings

Where would we be without zebra crossings?
Nipping in and out of the traffic jam
Jogging on the pavement waiting for take-off
Ready to sprint as soon as we can

Cross   Cross   I'm getting cross
Cross   Cross   I'm really cross
Cross   Cross   I'm going to cross
          Now!

Where would we be without zebra crossings?
Lost in space without the black and white path
Racing, pacing, twitching and itching
To reach the other side in the face of death

Cross   Cross   I walk across
Cross   Cross   Make drivers cross
Cross   Cross   Almost across
          Suddenly it's motocross!

Where would we be without zebra crossings?
Ask the mother with the kids in tow
Like a white flag on the battlefield
Waggle the pushchair and off they go

Cross   Cross   *She's getting cross*
Cross   Cross   *She's really cross*
Cross   Cross   *She's going to cross*
                Now!

Where would we be without zebra crossings?
Three big cheers for my old gran
Stick in hand she works her magic
Casting spells on white van man

Cross   Cross   Totters   across
Cross   Cross   Shows   who's   boss
Cross   Cross   Catches   her   bus

Bye Gran!

No Grannies in This Poem

There are no grannies in this poem
I wouldn't let one in if she tried
 It's no way to treat old ladies, I know
But I've kept them waiting outside

It's not raining there at the moment
And we are in for a settled spell
They've got lots of things to chatter about
And they get on reasonably well

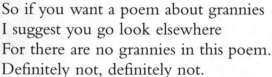

This poem, you see, is about witches
And subjects that grannies don't care for
Like vampires and aliens from outer space
Waging intergalactic warfare

So if you want a poem about grannies
I suggest you go look elsewhere
For there are no grannies in this poem.
Definitely not, definitely not.

Ructions

Ructions O'Rourke
is a pig with a mission
A mission to clean up
crime on the streets

Ruction's the name
for ructions he causes
When faced with liars
bullies and cheats

Trotters like tree trunks
a snout that will pulverize
Rotters and punks
who pull the wool over your eyes

Four hundred pounds
of muscular pork
His ambition to clean up
the streets of New York

Ructions O'Rourke
Ructions O'Rourke
A pig with a mission
is Ructions O'Rourke.

Fire Escapes

In old
New York
there are
fire escapes
every where.
□ Each
build ing
is girded
with black
iron girders.
□ Rungs
and ladders
going this
way and
that. □
Even the
fire escapes
have fire
escapes. □
What I
want to
know is
□ what
happens to
the fire
when it

escapes?

In Case of Fire

In case of fire break glass
In case of glass fill with water
In case of water fetch umbrella
In case of umbrella beware of Mary Poppins
In case of Mary Poppins switch off TV
In case of TV change channel
In case of Channel swim across
In case of cross say sorry
In case of sorry hold out arms
In case of arms lay down gun
In case of gun *Fire*
In case of fire break glass

Bees Cannot Fly

Bees cannot fly, scientists have proved it.
It is all to do with wingspan and body-weight.
Aerodynamically incapable of sustained flight,
Bees simply cannot fly. And yet they do.

There's one there, unaware of its dodgy ratios,
A noisy bubble, a helium-filled steamroller.
Fat and proud of it, buzzing about the garden
As if it were the last day of the spring sales.

Trying on all the brightest flowers, squeezing itself
Into frilly numbers three sizes too small.
Bees can fly, there's no need to prove it. And sting.
When stung, do scientists refuse to believe it?

Joy at the Sound

Joy at the silver birch in the morning sunshine
Joy at the spring-green of its fingertips

Joy at the swirl of cold milk in the blue bowl
Joy at the blink of its bubbles

Joy at the cat revving up on the lawn
Joy at the frogs that leapfrog to freedom

Joy at the screen as it fizzes to life
Joy at The Simpsons, Lisa and Bart

Joy at the dentist: 'Fine, see you next year'
Joy at the school gates: 'Closed'

Joy at the silver withholding the chocolate
Joy at the poem, two verses to go

Joy at the zing of the strings of the racquet
Joy at the bounce of the bright yellow ball

Joy at the key unlocking the door
Joy at the sound of her voice in the hall.

Icy Fingers

Despite the cold
A line of old trees
Playing with the moon

Tossing it
From one to the other
Never missing a catch.

Kettle Smocks

Kettle Smocks, Clocks and Watches, Stink Davie,
Fireflout, Lightning and Thundercup.
Neddy Grinnel, Granfer-Griggle, Tickling Tommy,
Hedgy-Pedgy, Yoe Brimble and Blindy Buff.

All of these have I seen today
As through the fields I made my way

Cuckoopint, Devil's Milk, Drunkard, Sleepyhead,
Lion's Tooth, Dog Choop, Cat Jug, Pig's Nose.
Plum Pudding and Pucky, Popple and Poppet,
Poppy, Red Campion, Dandelion, Briar Rose.

All of these have I seen today
(Or maybe not, for who is to say?)

49

The Casket

There is a broken casket
Washed up by the morning tide
With a young girl's magic mementoes
Trinkets and jewellery inside.

Letters from long-dead lovers
Tied now with a seaweed bow
A First World War photograph
Of a German matelot.

Two tickets for *Die Fledermaus*
Lie half-buried in the sand
And a poem by Christian Morgensten
Copied carefully by hand.

Attracted by the glittering
A hermit crab approaches
The casket's gaudy entrails
Of necklaces and brooches.

As the sun climbs high in the heavens
And fishermen return from the kill
The hermit crab scuttles for safety
As children swoop down from the hill.

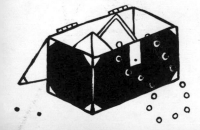

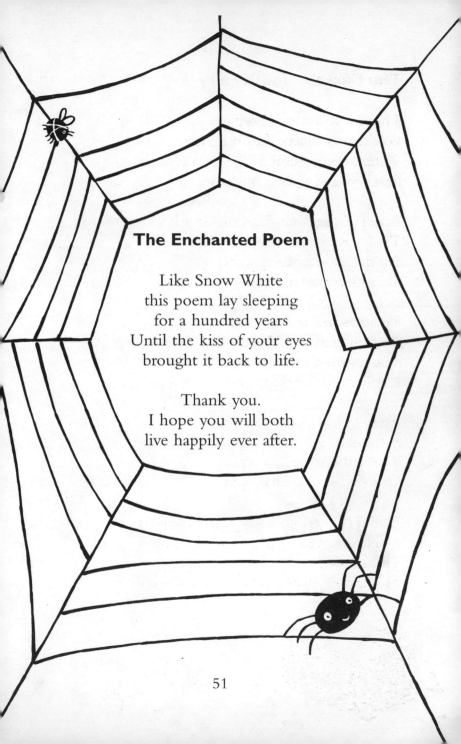

The Enchanted Poem

Like Snow White
this poem lay sleeping
for a hundred years
Until the kiss of your eyes
brought it back to life.

Thank you.
I hope you will both
live happily ever after.

Tears for the Tooth Fairy

The Tooth Fairy is crying.
Not tears of pain, but of disappointment.
Yesterday morning,
Not looking where she was flying
She flew straight into a toadstool
And knocked out her front tooth.

So, sleepy at bedtime
She put it under her pillow
Before turning off the light,
Made a wish and fell asleep.
And guess what? You're right.
This morning the tooth was still there!

The Hair Fairy

I'm going bald
And it's not fair
Where, oh where
Is the Fairy of Hair?

When I was young
And a tooth fell out
You didn't hear me
Weep or shout

For the Tooth Fairy
Would come to my aid
When fast asleep
I'd be well paid

If I got a pound
For each fallen hair
By now I'd be
A millionaire.

Millionaires Row

Millionaires row
Just like the rest of us

About the weather, and about how
to pronounce 'row'.

Pronunciation

'Where you come from,
is it pronounced
St Louey or St Louis?'

'Where I come from
it is pronounced
Chicago.'

The Corner

Rounding the corner
two men bumped into each other.
'Why don't you look where you're going?'
they chorused, side-stepped twice,
then hurried on.

Had there been an argument,
the corner
would have seen both sides of it.

Like a Fish

To say that she swims like a fish
Would not be doing her justice.
Fish can't do the breaststroke or butterfly
As gracefully as she can (although certain species
Are superior when it comes to the dolphin)

Admittedly, she can't stay underwater
For as long as fish can, nor can she eat
And sleep there. But then a fish
Doesn't smile when swimming
Or look half as sassy in a lycra swimsuit.

Like a Stone

To say that he sinks like a stone
Would not be doing him justice

Stones can't thresh about wildly
Bubble and splutter like him

Stones can't struggle out gasping,
'One day I'll learn how to swim.'

Cautionary Tale

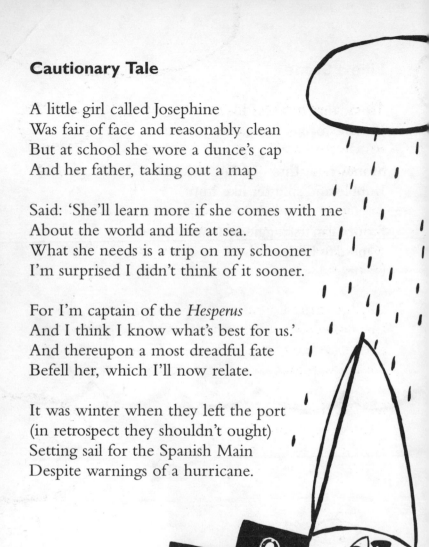

A little girl called Josephine
Was fair of face and reasonably clean
But at school she wore a dunce's cap
And her father, taking out a map

Said: 'She'll learn more if she comes with me
About the world and life at sea.
What she needs is a trip on my schooner
I'm surprised I didn't think of it sooner.

For I'm captain of the *Hesperus*
And I think I know what's best for us.'
And thereupon a most dreadful fate
Befell her, which I'll now relate.

It was winter when they left the port
(in retrospect they shouldn't ought)
Setting sail for the Spanish Main
Despite warnings of a hurricane.

Three days out there came the gale
Even the skipper he turned pale
And as for little Josephine
She turned seven shades of green

As the schooner rocked from port to starboard
Across the decks poor Josie scarpered
She ran from the fo'c'sle to the stern
(Some folks'll never learn)

Crying: 'Stop the boat, I want to go home,'
But unheeding, the angry foam
Swamped the decks. Her dad did curse
Knowing things would go from bad to worse

He called his daughter to his side
'Put on my seaman's coat,' he cried
'You'll be safe 'til the storm has passed,'
Then bound her tightly to the mast.

And pass it did, but sad to say
Not for a fortnight and a day.
By then the ship had foundered
And all the crew had drownded.

And reported later in the press
Was a story that caused much distress
Of a couple walking on the shore
And of the dreadful sight they saw

Tied to a mast, a few bones picked clean
All that remained of poor Josephine.

MORAL
Stay on at school, get your GCSEs
let others sail the seven seas.

Epitaphs

The Wreck of the Hesperus

A lass
bound
to a mast
Drowned
alas.

The Boy on the Burning Deck

The boy stood on
The burning deck
Jumped to safety
Broke his neck.

Lady Godiva

Here lies Lady Godiva
She didn't wear a bra
Or knickers iva.

Freak Tornado

Is tornado 'freak' as in 'unexpected'?
or 'freak' as in 'weird'?

As its arrival is always unexpected
then it must mean weird.

'Quickly, outside, everybody,
here comes a weird tornado!

Crazy! Two heads, purple skin,
and look at those bulging eyes!

Back into the house, everybody!
Oh, it's gone.'

Only a Dream?

I woke up, and it was only a dream.
With a huge sigh of relief, I got out of bed
and then I saw it, hovering in the corner ...

A skull dripping blood and green slime.
Its eye sockets staring, not at me,
but at some unspeakable horror beyond.

I turned and ran towards the door.
But too late. It slammed shut
locking me in from the outside.

As I tugged at the handle, it broke off
and became white-hot. I dropped it
on the carpet which burst into flames.

The smoke was acrid, burning. I staggered
across the room, hands over my eyes
and collapsed unconscious on the bed.

I woke up and it was only a dream.
With a huge sense of relief I got out of bed
and then I saw it, hovering in the corner ...

Limps

Limps lie around
occasionally in pairs
in wait for someone walking
completely unawares

At the sound of a footstep
they prick up their ears
licking their lips
as the victim appears

They whiplash the foot
as it passes by
then sink in their teeth
as you let out a cry

Holding fast to your ankle
they feed off the pain
as you stumble like someone
dragging a chain

And when at last the doctor
says, 'It's only a sprain'
they've scuttled off cackling
to lie in wait again

The Tongue-twister

Watch out for the dreaded Tongue-twister
When he pulls on his surgical gloves.
Keep your eyes open, your mouth tightly shut,
Twisting tongues is the thing that he loves.

It's the slippery, squirmy feel of them
As they wriggle like landed fish.
When he pulls and tugs and grapples
You'll gasp and gurgle and wish

That you'd never pulled tongues at teacher
Or a stranger behind their back,
As he twists out your tongue and pops it
Into his bobbling, twisted-tongue sack.

Scouse-power

They're scoffing scouse in Sydney
While surfing on Bondi Beach

In Rekjavik they like it thick
Lots of vodka within reach

There's tartan scouse in Inverness
Wi' whisky, neeps and tatties

In Bombay they add curry paste
And make sarnies with chapattis

A million clicking chopsticks
Mix the scouse with rice in China

Japanese guzzling sushi–scouse
Agree there's nothing finer

Spaniards no longer eat in fear
Of catching salmonella

Since they discovered how to make …
Olé … Scouse paella

The best Italian restaurants
Serve scouse-filled ravioli

In Rome, his holiness has blessed
Our dish and made it holy

And all across the USA
From Pittsburgh to 'Frisco Bay

From San José to Nantucket
Everyone has learned to cook it

So let's hear it now for SCOUSE!

*Scouse: A Merseyside dish of stewing steak and lamb,
carrots, onions and potatoes, brought to Liverpool by
Scandinavian sailors who called it* Labskause.

Michael Owen

Michael Owen, Michael Owen
When he kicks the ball
The ball keeps goin'

Through the net
And out of the ground
Michael Owen, sound as a pound.

I Have a Dream

I have a dream … about a football team
        wearing shirts of royal blue.
        Who win the League
        Who win the Cup
        Who conquer Europe too.

The team of the millennium!
But will my dream come true?
        My team, you see, is Everton,
        So much dreaming still to do.

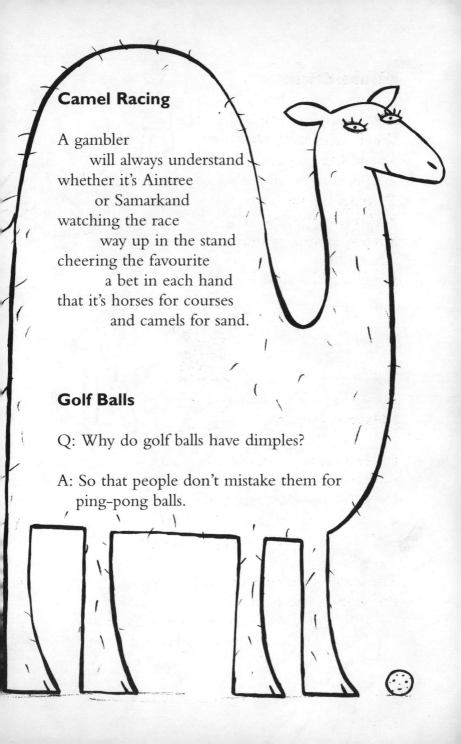

Camel Racing

A gambler
    will always understand
whether it's Aintree
    or Samarkand
watching the race
    way up in the stand
cheering the favourite
    a bet in each hand
that it's horses for courses
    and camels for sand.

Golf Balls

Q: Why do golf balls have dimples?

A: So that people don't mistake them for
    ping-pong balls.

A Day's Cricket

Before Tea:

Second slip
dropped a snick off the edge

Deep fine-leg
dropped a high lob

Silly mid-on
dropped a straight drive

During Tea:

Extra-cover
dropped a ham sandwich

Silly mid-wicket
dropped a beaker of orangeade

Square-leg
dropped a pair of trousers

After Tea:

Long-off
dropped a second beaker of fine
orangeade

Mid-off
dropped a deep-leg sandwich

The wicket-keeper
dropped an extra pair of silly square
trousers

Clocking Off

Stands the church clock at ten to eleven?
Sits the grandfather clock at half past one?
Jumps the alarm clock at five to seven?
Blinks the digital, then blank, time's gone!

On a Roll

'I'm on a roll! I'm on a roll!'
Said the fly on a hot dog.

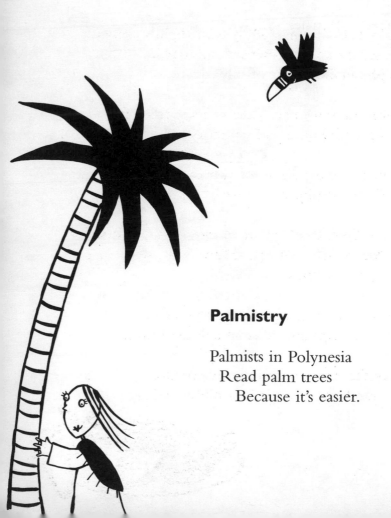

Palmistry

Palmists in Polynesia
  Read palm trees
    Because it's easier.

Rainbow Menu
(Durban, South Africa)

Overlooking the harbour on the twentieth floor
Breakfasting on food I've never tasted before

The fun is in mixing the exotic and unknown
With stuff that I'm familiar with at home

Streaky back bacon with banana, lightly grilled
Pork sausages with pawpaw and mango,
    slightly chilled

Smoked salmon slices with sweet pickled figs
Biltong with guava and scrambled eggs

Calamari, pineapple and I suppose a
Strawberry yoghurt goes well with samosa

If the waiters think me mad they don't let it show
'Another kipper with your kiwi fruit, sir?
    Just let me know.'

Biryani, salami and butternut squash
My platter a palette of multicoloured nosh

Lucky the poet composing this oration
On a rainbow menu in a rainbow nation.

Stage Fright

On arriving at the theatre there was no queue
So I bought a ticket and went straight to my seat.

When the house-lights faded and the curtain rose
I realized that I was the only one in the auditorium.

But it didn't matter because when the lights
Came up onstage … nothing happened.

For an hour or so I watched the empty space
Thinking, I am watching an empty space.

After a short interval the second half began
More of the same but, to my mind, even better.

When the final curtain fell, I jumped to my feet
And applauded. 'Author!' I cried, 'Author!'

As the applause died down, I climbed onstage
Took a bow, and with all due modesty,
Acknowledged the silence.

Taken at the Flood

'There is a tide in the affairs of men, which, if taken at the flood ...'
Shakespeare

Here is one of me taken at the flood
   My arm around my daughter
Seconds later the photographer slipped
   And fell into the water.

The Happy Angler

Laughing
all the way
to the bank.

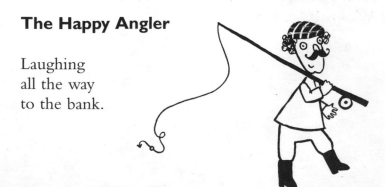

A Brush with Authority

I had a brush with authority
Not only did it tell me
What to paint and when
But also which colours to use.

Rubber Bullets

They sound harmless
But without a doubt
Rubber bullets
Rub people out.

Give and Take

I give you clean air
You give me poisonous gas.
I give you mountains
You give me quarries.

I give you pure snow
You give me acid rain.
I give you spring fountains
You give me toxic canals.

I give you a butterfly
You gave me a plastic bottle.
I give you a blackbird
You gave me a stealth bomber.

I give you abundance
You give me waste.
I give you one last chance
You give me excuse after excuse.

Love Poem

If words were feelings
This poem would put its arms around you

Memories

she loves him
she loves him not
she loves him
she loves him not

she leaves him
and all he's got
are memories
that hurt a lot

Trunk Call

In parts of Southern Spain it was the custom
of women who needed to get in touch
with their husbands working in the fields
some distance away, to approach an olive tree
and whisper into a hole in its trunk.

The message was usually received and the men
would carry out whatever task was required.
When one of the women was asked why she used
a tree, she replied, 'Because I am poor,
If I were rich I would use a telephone.'

A Ring

'Give me a ring,' said Amanda
To the boy she met on a train
'Sure thing,' said Harry, excited
At the thought of seeing her again

So he telephoned next morning
And they chatted till late afternoon
Then she rang back in the evening
And they talked the light off the moon

They talked the hind legs off donkeys
They talked the leaves off the trees
They talked the sheep off the hillsides
They talked the wind off the seas

They talked the colours off rainbows
They talked the carpets off floors
They talked the chimneys off rooftops
They talked the numbers off doors

They talked the laces off trainers
They talked the diamonds off crowns
They talked the skins off bananas
They talked the noses off clowns

They talked the witches off broomsticks
They talked the whiskers off cats
They'd have talked till the Last Trumpet sounded
Had phone bills not dropped on their mats

'Give me a ring,' said Amanda
'Hip hip,' said Harry, 'hooray!'
And with the cash they'd have squandered
Got married the following day.

I Married a Human Cannonball

I married a human cannonball
Against my mother's wishes
One day he went ballistic
And started throwing dishes

So I left him for a fire-eater
Who, inflamed with wild desire
Kissed me once so passionately
He set my hair on fire

Then I fell for a hypnotist
And his irresistible spell
But my life as a chicken
Became a living hell

So I left him for a strong man
Who pulled tractors with his teeth
But when he took them out at night
He thpoke all thoft like thith

A clown moved in to make me laugh
Red nose and criss-cross eyes
But he never took his make-up off
And oh, those custard pies

So I ran away from the circus
Joined the convent as a nun
No slapstick, crowds or greasepaint
Oh, so quiet, but much more fun.

Lullaby

No monsters are hiding under the bed
    I give you my word
The idea of vampires thirsting for blood
    Is plainly absurd

There are no such things as ghosts I promise
    They're all in the mind
Headless horsemen, hobgoblins and aliens
    All nonsense you'll find

You will not fall under a witch's spell
    You are not Snow White
Nor am I a handsome prince, but still
    A kiss, God bless, good night.

Riddlediddle

I hang from a silver thread
     and flourish between pleasure and pain
I give freedom
     and turn the street into a swollen river
I come from the fields
     and enter your house grinning in a sack
I cover your table
     and touch your face when darkness falls
I am a swift scribble
     and when glowing I tremble like a hill
I am cuddle-shaped
     and yet I slide silkenly from your grasp
I am a smile that listened
     and came away tired but none the wiser
I am the thought
     and when needed will meet you halfway
What am I?

Index of First Lines

Answers to riddles:

Page 36 (i) Eyes
        (ii) Milestone

Page 85 Your guess is as good as mine!